Visual Geography Series®

PANAMA

...in Pictures

Prepared by
Geography Department

Lerner Publications Company
Minneapolis

Courtesy of United Nations

Children play near their makeshift homes that are gradually being replaced with better residences.

This is an all-new edition of the Visual Geography
Series. Previous editions have been published by
Sterling Publishing Company, New York City, and
some of the original textual information has been re-
tained. New photographs, maps, charts, captions, and
updated information have been added. The text has
been entirely reset in 10/12 Century Textbook.

LIBRARY OF CONGRESS CATALOGING-IN-PUBLICATION DATA

Panama in pictures.

(Visual geography series)
Rev. ed. of: Panama and the Canal Zone in pictures /
prepared by Peter English.
Includes index.
Summary: An introduction to the geography, history,
government, people, economy, and culture of the
Republic of Panama and the Panama Canal.
1. Panama. 2. Panama Canal (Panama) [1. Panama.
2. Panama Canal (Panama)]   I. English, Peter. Panama
and the Canal Zone in pictures.   II. Lerner Publications
Company. III. Series: Visual geography series (Min-
neapolis, Minn.)
F1563.P325   1987   972.87   86–33786
ISBN 0–8225–1818–X (lib. bdg.)

International Standard Book Number: 0–8225–1818–X
Library of Congress Catalog Card Number: 86–33786

VISUAL GEOGRAPHY SERIES®

Publisher
Harry Jonas Lerner
Associate Publisher
Nancy M. Campbell
Executive Series Editor
Mary M. Rodgers
Editorial Assistant
Nora W. Kniskern
Illustrations Editor
Nathan A. Haverstock
Consultants/Contributors
Dr. Ruth F. Hale
Nathan A. Haverstock
Sandra K. Davis
Designer
Jim Simondet
Cartographer
Carol F. Barrett
Indexer
Kristine S. Schubert
Production Manager
Richard J. Hannah

Courtesy of Inter-American Development Bank

**Workers assemble scaffolding in preparation for the res-
toration of *Las Bóvedas,* an old Spanish fort.**

Acknowledgments

Title page photo courtesy of Leanne Hogie.

Elevation contours adapted from *The Times Atlas of
the World,* seventh comprehensive edition (New York:
Times Books, 1985).

3   4   5   6   7   8   9   10   96   95   94   93   92   91   90   89

Among the ruins of Old Panama, dancers perform the "Devil's Dance," which is famous in the province of Los Santos in southern Panama.

Contents

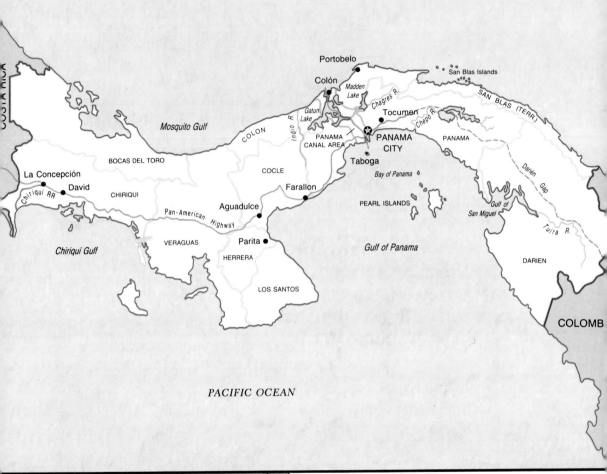

REPUBLIC OF PANAMA

N

—— Province Boundaries

—— Panama Canal Area Boundaries

0 ————— 50 Miles

0 ————— 50 Kilometers

CARIBBEAN SEA

COSTA RICA

Portobelo

Colón

San Blas Islands

Madden Lake

Chagres R.

SAN BLAS (TERR.)

Gatun Lake

Indio R.

Tocumen

Chepo R.

Mosquito Gulf

COLON

PANAMA CANAL AREA

PANAMA CITY

PANAMA

Darién Gap

BOCAS DEL TORO

Taboga

Bay of Panama

COCLE

La Concepción

David

Farallon

Gulf of San Miguel

Turra R.

CHIRIQUI

Chiriquí RR

Pan-American Highway

Aguadulce

PEARL ISLANDS

DARIEN

Chiriquí Gulf

VERAGUAS

Parita

Gulf of Panama

HERRERA

COLOMB

LOS SANTOS

PACIFIC OCEAN

105°   90°

30°

GULF OF MEXICO

PACIFIC

OCEAN

CARIBBEAN

15°

SEA

PANAMA

MIDDLE AMERICA

PACIFIC

OCEAN

500   1000 Miles

0   500   1000 Kilometers

EQUATOR   0°

METRIC CONVERSION CHART
To Find Approximate Equivalents

WHEN YOU KNOW:	MULTIPLY BY:	TO FIND:
AREA		
acres	0.41	hectares
square miles	2.59	square kilometers
CAPACITY		
gallons	3.79	liters
LENGTH		
feet	30.48	centimeters
yards	0.91	meters
miles	1.61	kilometers
MASS (weight)		
pounds	0.45	kilograms
tons	0.91	metric tons
VOLUME		
cubic yards	0.77	cubic meters
TEMPERATURE		
degrees Fahrenheit	0.56 (*after* subtracting 32)	degrees Celsius

Pots and jars of many sizes catch the eye of visitors to Panama, where the quality of locally produced earthenware is well known.

Introduction

On January 1, 1990, two members of the Panama Canal Commission will switch jobs. The Panamanian who will have been deputy administrator until that date will take charge of the Panama Canal, and the U.S. citizen who will have been in charge will become the deputy administrator. Treaties between the United States and Panama that became effective in 1979 provide for a careful transition of authority over the Panama Canal and the Canal Area (the strip of territory through which the canal passes). Panama will assume sole sovereignty over the canal and its operation by 1999. After that date, the United States may intervene militarily only if there is a threat to the neutrality of the canal.

Panama, once a remote province of Colombia, owes its nationhood to the canal. For Panamanians, control of the small waterway means control over their national destiny.

Although the canal is Panama's greatest economic asset, it is aging. It has become too shallow and narrow for some supertankers and warships. In addition, the number of ships using the canal is declining, partly because of competition from other modes of transportation. A pipeline across Panama, for example, allows oil to be pumped from ocean to ocean between supertankers too big to fit through the canal. Determined to remain an international crossroads, Panama is considering whether it should widen the existing canal or even build an entirely new sea-level canal.

The country is also moving to improve other national assets. The completion of a highway across the jungles and swamps of eastern Panama will provide the first land passage between North and South America. Except for the Darién Gap— an unfinished stretch near the Panama-Colombia border—the Pan-American Highway is complete. Once the 100-mile gap has been closed, motorists will be able to travel by road from Fairbanks, Alaska, to Punta Arenas, Chile, at the southern tip of South America.

Panama's strategic importance was realized in 1513. In that year, the Spaniard Vasco Núñez de Balboa and his fellow explorers climbed a mountain in the Darién jungles to become the first Europeans to glimpse the Atlantic and Pacific oceans from a single point. Soon thereafter, Panama flourished as the place where the treasures from the rich mines of Peru were loaded aboard fleets bound for Spain. Seventeenth-century pirates eventually made Panama an unsafe place to store goods for shipment to Spain. As a result, the narrow isthmus became little more than a ne-

Courtesy of Panama Canal Commission

A ship entering the Panama Canal from the Pacific side passes under Puente de las Américas, which forms part of the Pan-American Highway system.

glected province of New Granada (later Colombia).

In the 1840s the United States—as well as several European countries—became interested in building a canal to connect the oceans. A French attempt to build a canal failed in the 1880s. By the turn of the century, the United States had assumed the engineering job. Begun in 1906, the enormous excavation and construction feats were completed in 1914. The low-paid labor force consisted largely of Caribbean black people—called Antilleans—who have yet to become an accepted part of Panamanian society.

For almost 75 years, the canal has offered international vessels a sea-lane between the oceans. Initially, much of the profits for this service went to the United States. Later adjustments have given more of the canal's revenues to Panama.

In the late 1980s, Panama became a focus of U.S. efforts to stem the flow of illegal drugs from South America to the United States. The U.S. Drug Enforcement Administration accused the head of Panama's military forces, General Manuel Noriega, of making Panama a base for the distribution of cocaine and marijuana. As a result of investigations, a U.S. court charged and convicted Noriega of drug trafficking.

To further show its discontent with Noriega's activities, the U.S. government also imposed economic penalties, called sanctions, on Panama. The United States hoped that the sanctions would force the general to give up his authority and to leave Panama. Noriega, however, continued to run Panama in 1988.

The sanctions have contributed to major decreases in the nation's economic activity and to high unemployment rates. Noriega has responded to the economic penalties and to internal attempts to depose him by crushing political opposition in Panama. Even if Panamanians can resolve the current crisis, they face a long period of economic and political recovery.

A rushing stream in Chiriquí province, western Panama, is one of many small waterways throughout the nation.

Valerio Hernández, a farmer who has recently settled in the newly opened areas of Darién province in eastern Panama, waits for a truck to convey his corn to market in Piriatí.

7

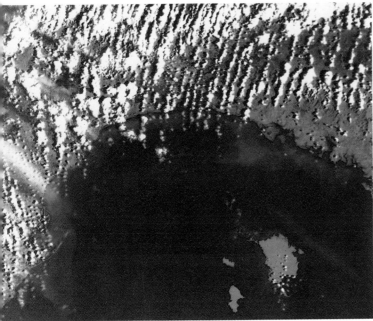

In a satellite view of Panama, the color red indicates forested areas, while offshore the Pearl Islands are visible. Panama City is on the mainland to the right of the white streak, which represents the Panama Canal.

1) The Land

The Republic of Panama snakes between the two giant continents of North and South America. The Caribbean Sea—an arm of the Atlantic Ocean—is to the north, and the Pacific Ocean is to the south. Colombia, Panama's former overseer and its link to South America, lies to the east. Costa Rica is situated to the west of Panama and connects Panama to the rest of North America. The republic has an area of 29,762 square miles, including the 553 square miles of the Panama Canal Area. The greatest east-west distance in the country is 450 miles, and the greatest north-south distance is 130 miles.

Topography

Most of Panama is covered by wooded hills and low mountain ranges. Rising near the Costa Rican border, extinct Barú Volcano (11,410 feet) is the country's highest peak and was once known as Mount Chiriquí. From this peak, the mountains of the Serranía de Tabasará slope to a region of low hills near the middle of the country—the site of the Panama Canal. East of the canal, the Cordillera de San Blas and Serranía del Darién hug the north coast and gradually rise to more than 7,000 feet near the Colombian border. These two ranges are part of the Andes Mountains, which stretch down the length of South America.

Fertile plains and valleys lie between the mountains and the coasts. Most of Panama's population live on the Pacific coast, between the canal and the Costa Rican border. Thick jungles cover much of the eastern part of the country, and some parts of this region are uninhabitable.

Coastline and Rivers

Panama's Caribbean coast is 426 miles long, and its largest indentation is the Mosquito Gulf. The 767-mile-long Pacific coast is more deeply hollowed, and the Chiriquí and Panama gulfs are the largest bays on the Pacific side. About 1,600 small islands, mostly in the San Blas and Pearl archipelagoes (island groups), lie off both of Panama's coasts.

Of Panama's more than 300 rivers, those that flow into the Pacific Ocean are longer, slower running, and have larger basins than the waterways of the Atlantic slopes. The nation's only navigable river is the Tuira, which empties into the Gulf of San Miguel. The second longest river, the Chepo in Panama province, is the site of a major hydroelectric complex.

The Pacific shoreline is shallow and has tides in excess of 12 feet, with wide mud-flats extending seaward from the shore. The Caribbean coastline, on the other hand, has several good natural harbors,

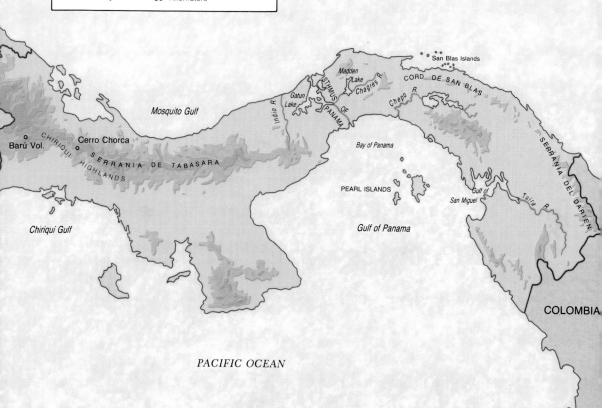

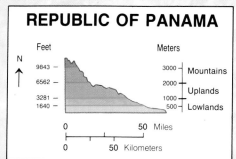

REPUBLIC OF PANAMA

Feet / Meters

9843 — 3000 Mountains
6562 — 2000
3281 — 1000 Uplands
1640 — 500 Lowlands

N

0   50 Miles
0   50 Kilometers

CARIBBEAN SEA

San Blas Islands

Madden Lake
Chagres R.
CORD. DE SAN BLAS
Gatun Lake
ISTHMUS OF PANAMA
Chepo R.
Indio R.
Mosquito Gulf

Barú Vol.
Cerro Chorca
CHIRIQUÍ HIGHLANDS
SERRANIA DE TABASARA

Bay of Panama

SERRANIA DEL DARIEN

Chiriquí Gulf

PEARL ISLANDS
Gulf of San Miguel
Tuira R.

Gulf of Panama

COLOMBIA

PACIFIC OCEAN

but few towns. The only important seaport facilities in this area are at Cristobal, near the Atlantic end of the canal.

Climate

Because Panama lies near the equator, temperatures are uniformly high, and there is little seasonal change except in rainfall. Temperatures in the lowlands average about 80° F throughout the year, and humidity is always high. Mountain temperatures average 66° F but sometimes drop to 50° F. The Atlantic side of the country receives about 130 inches of rain a year. Only about half as much rain (68 inches) falls on the Pacific side annually, and some regions are subject to drought. Insufficient rainfall especially affects areas that front the western shores of the Gulf of Panama, such as the provinces of Los Santos and Coclé. On the

Pacific coast, seasons are defined in terms of rainfall—a short dry season and a longer rainy one. The rainy period continues from April through December, while January, February, and March are relatively dry. An average of less than two inches of precipitation falls during these three dry months.

Natural Resources

The principal natural resource of Panama is the fertile soil of its valleys and plains. In addition, rich forests cover most of the country, with mahogany stands being common in the eastern regions. The mountains of eastern Panama contain small deposits of gold. Vast reserves of copper have been found at Cerro Colorado in the mountains of Chiriquí province and, if developed, could become one of the largest mining operations in the world. Cop-

Efforts to complete the Pan-American Highway have opened up eastern Panama's richly forested lands to hardwood logging operations.

per has also been discovered at Petaquilla, Cerro Chorca, and Rio Pinto. Large coal reserves have been found near Rio Indio. Other minerals in Panama include manganese, iron, mercury, and silver. Limestone for cement manufacturing is abundant, as is shale for the production of bricks and tiles.

Shrimp, pearl oysters, and many kinds of fish live in the coastal waters. Shrimp farms, located near Aguadulce on the Pacific coast, have helped to make shrimp Panama's third largest export.

Flora and Fauna

Situated where North and South America meet, Panama has a considerable range of plants and animals. In general, however, South American types predominate.

Palm trees are common at sea level, and mangroves thrive in the coastal swamps. Hardwood forests cover the lowlands and plateaus. At higher altitudes, there are

Independent Picture Service

The *Peristeria elata,* or Holy Spirit orchid, is Panama's national flower and blooms in August and September.

mixed forests where conifers—especially pines—share space with the hardwood trees.

Pumas, jaguars, and white-tailed deer are among the large animals found in Panama. Smaller forms include monkeys, many kinds of rodents and reptiles, armadillos, otters, opossums, and a great variety of birds and insects.

Provinces and Cities

Panama is divided into nine provinces that range in population from Panama province with about one million inhabitants to Darién with about 30,000 residents. The other provinces, in descending order of population, are Chiriquí, Veraguas, Colón, Coclé, Herrera, Los Santos, and Bocas del Toro. The nation also includes one territory, San Blas, which is usually treated as part of Colón in most official documents. San Blas is inhabited predominantly by Cuna Indians, one of the country's three major Indian groups.

Courtesy of United Nations

A workman weighs a batch of small shrimp caught in Panama's coastal waters.

Panama City dates from the late seventeenth century, when the capital was moved five miles west of the site that was destroyed by a pirate raid in 1671.

The republic has roughly 70 cities and towns, which range in population from the capital city of Panamá—called Panama City in English—with a total of 652,000 residents, to Taboga with only 1,500 inhabitants. Panama City—founded in 1519 by the Spaniard Pedro Arias Dávila—lies at the Pacific end of the canal.

More than half of Panama's people live in urban areas. About 85 percent of these city dwellers reside in the two cities at the ends of the canal—Panama City, with its growing suburb of San Miguelito, and Colón.

The Panama Canal Area

Just after achieving its independence from Colombia in 1903, Panama signed an agreement with the United States to establish the Panama Canal Zone. Since ratification of the 1977 Panama Canal treaties, which returned control of the zone to the Panamanians, this region has been renamed the Panama Canal Area. The canal itself runs through the middle of the 10-mile-wide strip that extends between the Atlantic and Pacific oceans. The Canal Area covers 553 square miles, including 191 square miles of water.

Under the 1903 agreements, the United States was given the right to build and operate the Panama Canal and to govern the zone using Balboa Heights as its administrative headquarters. Later agreements added Madden Lake, northeast of the canal, and Trinidad Bay, in the southwest, to U.S. jurisdiction. The United States never governed Panama City or Colón, even though they were at opposite ends of the zone under U.S. control.

The Panama Canal

The Panama Canal crosses the Isthmus of Panama—a long, narrow strip of land that links North and South America. This land bridge between the two continents does not run in a north-to-south direction but rather is a west-to-east connection. Because of this confusion, compass directions are rarely used in Panama. Instead, references are made to the Atlantic or the Pacific side.

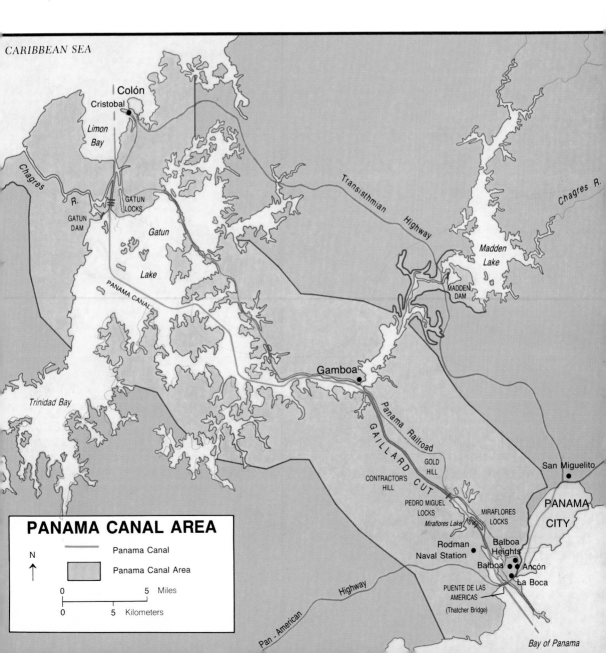

PANAMA CANAL AREA

N ↑

— Panama Canal

▨ Panama Canal Area

0 — 5 Miles

0 — 5 Kilometers

CARIBBEAN SEA

Colón
Cristobal
Limon Bay
Chagres R.
GATUN LOCKS
GATUN DAM
Gatun Lake
PANAMA CANAL
Trinidad Bay
Transisthmian Highway
Madden Lake
Chagres R.
MADDEN DAM
Gamboa
Panama Railroad
Panama Canal
GAILLARD CUT
GOLD HILL
CONTRACTOR'S HILL
PEDRO MIGUEL LOCKS
Miraflores Lake
MIRAFLORES LOCKS
San Miguelito
PANAMA CITY
Rodman Naval Station
Balboa Heights
Balboa
Ancón
La Boca
PUENTE DE LAS AMERICAS
(Thatcher Bridge)
Highway
Pan - American
Bay of Panama

Looking south from the west bank of the former Culebra Cut, a steam shovel is hard at work in June 1914. In the distance dredging boats handle a mud slide.

Since each ship uses about 50 million gallons of water, there is a great need for additional reservoirs. Madden Dam, built to serve this purpose in 1934, is located several miles up the Chagres River.

The United States built the 50-mile-long canal between 1906 and 1914. Thousands of laborers worked to construct the waterway, removing 211 million cubic yards of earth and rock in the process. The builders of the canal used steam shovels and dredges to cut through jungles, hills, and swamps. In addition to the many engineering problems they solved, the U.S. team also conquered several tropical diseases that had taken the lives of many workers. To achieve all this, the United States spent more than $300 million.

In order to raise and lower ships from one level to another, the canal has three sets of locks, or water-filled chambers. The locks were built in pairs to allow ships to pass through the canal in both directions at the same time. Each lock has a usable length of 1,000 feet, a width of 110 feet, and a depth of about 70 feet. The dimensions of the locks limit the size of ships that can pass through the waterway. Supercarriers, as well as many large civilian oil tankers and cargo ships, are too wide to use the canal.

Independent Picture Service

By using Trask's tank brush to apply a bug killer, a worker attempts to control the mosquitoes in a ditch at the time of the construction of the canal.

Furthermore, the canal itself runs diagonally northwest to southeast across the isthmus, from Limon Bay on the Atlantic side to the Bay of Panama on the Pacific side. A ship sailing from the Atlantic to the Pacific actually exits the canal 27 miles east of where it entered.

Until the canal was built, a ship traveling from New York City to San Francisco faced a journey of more than 13,000 miles. Such a trip required that the vessel, after sailing down the eastern coast of the United States, travel farther south along the Atlantic coast of South America, rounding the continent's tip at Cape Horn. The ship would then sail northward along the southern continent's Pacific coast before finally reaching the west coast of the United States. The canal shortened this journey by about 7,800 miles and by many days.

A Trip Through the Canal

A ship sailing into the canal from the Atlantic Ocean enters through Limon Bay, the inlet leading to the port of Cristobal in the Canal Area. While the ship is still in deep water, a canal pilot comes on board from a small boat. The pilot has charge of the ship during its trip through the canal. After passing through the breakwater at the entrance to the bay, the ship proceeds south along the seven-mile-long channel that leads to the Gatun Locks. The shipyards, docks, and fueling stations of Cristobal line the eastern shore of the bay.

GATUN LOCKS

The Gatun Locks system, which resembles a giant stairway, is made of three pairs of concrete chambers. They help to lift ships that are entering from the Atlantic side from sea level to Gatun Lake—a

15

distance of 85 feet. Small electric locomotives, called mules, run on tracks along both sides of the locks and, with cables, pull ships through the chambers. The locomotives ascend an incline at the end of each chamber to reach the next, higher level. This procedure allows the same set of locomotives to pull ships through the entire length of the Gatun Locks. Depending on the vessel's size, 4 to 12 locomotives are used for each ship.

As the ship approaches the first chamber, its engines are shut off, and canal workers attach the ship to the locomotives' towing cables. The locomotives then pull the ship into the first chamber, as huge steel gates close behind the vessel. Canal workers open valves that allow water from Gatun Lake to flow into the chamber through openings in the bottom of the lock. During the next 15 minutes, the rising water gradually lifts the ship. When the level of the water is the same as the level in the second chamber, the gates in front of the ship swing outward, and the locomotives pull the vessel into the second

chamber. Again the water level is raised. The process is repeated until the third chamber of the locks raises the ship to the level of Gatun Lake, which covers over 160 square miles of area.

GATUN LAKE

Next, canal workers release the cables, and the raised ship sails out of the locks under its own power. As it heads south across Gatun Lake, it passes huge Gatun Dam to the west of the locks. The ship steams across the lake from the Gatun Locks to Gamboa, following the 22-mile-long channel that was once the Chagres River Valley. The formerly lush river valley was almost completely covered by water when engineers flooded the area to create Gatun Lake. Long, coarse stems of water hyacinths, which have green leaves and violet blossoms, float on the surface of the lake. These plants become entangled in the propellers of ships and can endanger navigation. A hyacinth patrol destroys millions of the flowers each year to keep the channel clear.

Independent Picture Service

Ships proceed both north and south through the three concrete water chambers of the Gatun Locks. Over a distance of 1.2 miles, the locks either lift vessels 85 feet to the level of Gatun Lake to enter the canal or lower them to exit the waterway.

A northern view of the Culebra Cut in late 1906 shows evidence of a recent flood—one of many that had slowed work progress.

GAILLARD CUT

When the ship reaches the southeastern end of Gatun Lake, it enters the 8-mile-long, 500-foot-wide Gaillard Cut, which has a minimum depth of 42 feet. *Cut* is an engineering term for an artificial passageway or channel. Originally called the Culebra Cut, the Gaillard Cut runs between Gold Hill on the east and Contractor's Hill on the west. In 1913 it was renamed in honor of David Du Bose Gaillard, the engineer in charge of digging between the hills. Dredgers work constantly to keep the channel clear of earthslides. In some years, the dredgers in the Gaillard Cut remove as much as one million cubic yards of fallen earth.

PEDRO MIGUEL AND MIRAFLORES LOCKS

After the ship steams out of the Gaillard Cut, electric locomotives pull it into the Pedro Miguel Locks. These locks lower the vessel 31 feet in one step to Miraflores Lake. The ship sails one and a half miles

across the lake to the Miraflores Locks. Here, two chambers lower the vessel to the level of the Pacific Ocean. The distance that these chambers must lower the ship depends on the height of the Pacific tides. Tides at the Pacific end of the canal rise and fall about 12.5 feet twice a day. Tides on the Atlantic side change only about two feet daily.

Once out of the locks, the ship heads down the eight-mile-long channel between the Miraflores Locks and the end of the canal. The vessel passes the houses and buildings of the towns of Balboa, Balboa Heights, and La Boca that stand on the shores of the channel. The ship travels under Puente de las Américas (also called Thatcher Bridge)—an important link in the Pan-American Highway—and the pilot disembarks. The ship then enters the Bay of Panama and steams toward the open sea. The vessel has traveled a little over 50 miles from the Atlantic to the Pacific in about eight hours.

Independent Picture Service

The Culebra Cut was renamed the Gaillard Cut after Colonel David Du Bose Gaillard who was the engineer in charge of its construction. The engineering feat required that workers cut through eight miles of volcanic rock.

Photo by Meg and Don Malde Arnosti

By using the navigation aids on the hillsides, a Korean tanker christened *Viking Tern* makes its way through the Gaillard Cut.

The Atlantic-bound *Viking Tern* enters the Pedro Miguel Locks having made its way from the Pacific side via the Miraflores Locks.

The refurbished World War II battleship *Iowa* leaves the Miraflores Locks, which have the highest lock gates in the canal system because of the extreme tidal variation in the Pacific Ocean.

When the Spanish conquistadors arrived, the Cuna Indians fled to the remote San Blas Islands of northern Panama. Here, descendants of the Cuna still live simple lives—building their own dugout canoes; dwelling in small, round homes; and remaining distant from the mainland.

2) History and Government

Three main groups of Indians lived in Panama before the arrival of the Europeans. The Guaymí, related to members of the Maya and Nahua nations of Mexico and Central America, resided in the highlands along the present-day Costa Rican border. The Chocó, members of the Chibcha people who are found in modern Colombia, lived in western parts of Panama. The Cuna were skillful potters, stonecutters, and artists who fled to the remote San Blas Islands off Panama's northern coast when the Spanish arrived. All of these peoples dwelt in circular, thatched homes and shared the work of planting and harvesting the vegetables and fruits that formed part of their diets.

Arrival of the Spanish

The voyages of Christopher Columbus in the late fifteenth century fired the imaginations of many other explorers, including the Spaniard Rodrigo de Bastidas. In 1501

Bastidas sailed west from Venezuela in search of gold and landed in northern Panama. As a result of his explorations, Spain sent colonists to Panama (which it then called Darién) in 1509 and established settlements along the Caribbean coast.

The Indians did not welcome the arrival of the Spaniards, who enslaved many of the area's original inhabitants. Others died of European diseases against which they had no natural protection. The Indians who escaped disease and Spanish enslavement fled into the forests.

Vasco Núñez de Balboa, a member of Bastidas's crew, had been elected to ad-minister the settlements in Darién in 1510. He encouraged the Spaniards to plant crops in order to become more self-sufficient and, after raiding some Indian communities, also tried to befriend the local inhabitants. They told Balboa about a large sea where gold might be found.

In 1513 Balboa and nearly 200 Spaniards blazed a trail through the central and southern parts of the colony in search of riches. Instead of finding gold, they became the first Europeans to see both the Atlantic and Pacific oceans from one vantage point. Upon his return in 1514, Balboa was told that the Spanish had replaced him

The Spanish conquistador Vasco Núñez de Balboa was the first European to travel across the Isthmus of Panama and to see both the Atlantic and Pacific oceans. Balboa, governor of Darién (as Panama was once called) in 1511, was the victim of intrigues at the Spanish court and lost his post to Pedro Arias Dávila, who accused Balboa of treason and had him beheaded.

After the Spanish arrived in Panama in the sixteenth century, they put the local inhabitants to work as forced laborers.

Courtesy of James Ford Bell Library, University of Minnesota

with a rival explorer named Pedro Arias Dávila. Wanting to discredit Balboa completely, the new governor charged Balboa with treason and ordered him to be executed in 1517.

Panama's Economic Rise

Given full control of the colony, Dávila decided to build its capital. In 1519 he chose a small fishing village on which to establish a new city. The local Indians called the place *Panama,* meaning "plenty of fish," and here Dávila founded Panama City. A road connected Panama City on the Pacific to Nombre de Dios—a Spanish port on the Caribbean. Treasures from the Incan civilization in Peru and from other cultures throughout the Americas passed along this route. Once the goods reached

By the mid-sixteenth century, Panama was a major trading port for goods and looted treasures shipped to Spain.

Photo by Bettmann Archive

22

Nombre de Dios, the Spanish loaded them onto ships headed for Spain.

In an effort to control trade between Spain and its colonies, the Spanish government issued strict commercial decrees. These laws forbade direct contact between foreign traders and Spanish colonists. The decrees allowed only three ports—Nombre de Dios, Cartagena (in Colombia), and Veracruz (in Mexico)—to exchange goods with Spain or with other European powers.

For decades, gold and silver were carried overland to Nombre de Dios on the Caribbean Sea and then shipped to Spain. Eventually, the Spanish allowed Portobelo, another harbor on Panama's section of the Caribbean coastline, to develop into a huge trading station.

The colony prospered or declined with the flow of goods into its ports. The exhaustion of Incan gold, for example, brought a decrease in commercial activity, while the discovery of Peruvian silver increased shipments to Spain and enhanced Panama's importance.

The Audiencia of Panama

In 1538, as evidence of Panama's importance in Spanish affairs, the colony became the seat of an audiencia (court). Spain organized all of its colonial territory—from Nicaragua in Central America to Chile in South America—under the authority of Panama. This arrangement lasted only until 1543, when Spain realized that the audiencia was far too large for effective administration. A decree in 1563 gave Panama its own audiencia but put it under the control of a larger administrative unit called the Viceroyalty of Peru.

In addition to settlers and officials, Spain sent Roman Catholic missionaries to Panama. They converted some of the local inhabitants to Christianity and curbed the

Courtesy of David Mangurian

Compañía de Jesús Church, founded in 1519, now lies in ruins in Casco Antiguo, about three miles from the modern capital of Panama City.

abuses of the settlers, who had been using the Indians as slave laborers. Nevertheless, slavery continued, and many of the region's original peoples fled to unreachable parts of the colony to escape capture. A labor shortage resulted, and Spain began to send enslaved Africans to replace the dwindling numbers of Indian workers.

Panama's Economic Decline

In the seventeenth century, piracy began to affect the fortunes of Panama. With bulging storehouses and with money-laden ships in its ports, Panama was an attractive prize for buccaneers. To avoid the pirates, ships sailed around Cape Horn at the southern tip of South America and then headed for Spain. The Englishman Francis Drake raided Nombre de Dios in the late sixteenth century, paving the way for other pirates to attack the colony. Welsh buccaneer Henry Morgan sacked

Courtesy of New York Public Library

Henry Morgan, a Welshman from Llanrhymny, began his career as the captain of a pirate ship in 1666. Tried in 1672 for sacking the Panamanian capital, he not only was acquitted of the charges but was knighted by his sovereign, Britain's King Charles II. The king later appointed Morgan to be lieutenant governor of Jamaica—the island that served as the Welsh pirate's base of operations.

Courtesy of New York Public Library

Pirates of the seventeenth and eighteenth centuries knew that Portobelo's treasure house (called the King's Storehouse) held the gold taken from Peru until it could be shipped to Spain in convoy. Thus, the port became the target of many attacks. Henry Morgan sacked it en route to Panama City, and Britain's Admiral Edward Vernon blasted it with canonfire in the eighteenth century.

24

Panama City in 1671 at the request of the British governor of Jamaica.

Along with piracy, smuggling contributed to Panama's shrinking importance as a trading center. Because Spain controlled the flow of goods into Panama, Great Britain, France, and the Netherlands smuggled their trade items into other ports in the colony. Illegal trade flourished to the point where legal exchanges almost vanished. By 1739 Panama's commercial position had declined so much that Spain weakened the colony's internal authority and made it a part of the Viceroyalty of New Granada (later Colombia).

By 1740 Spain had discontinued the laws that had prevented the direct exchange of goods between Spanish colonists and European merchants. This change

Independent Picture Service

Attacks on Panama City in the seventeenth century eventually took their toll on the colonial port. All that remains of the cathedral in the old part of the city is the tall bell tower.

Courtesy of James H. Marrinan

This New World coin was minted in 1756 and carries the coat of arms of the Bourbon monarchs of Spain. They ruled the colonies of Spanish America until the nineteenth century.

benefited Spain but drove Panama deeper into its economic decline because the colony had long been dependent on trade with Spain to make money. When Spanish ships were allowed to go to any port, Panama lost much of its traffic and, therefore, its main means of collecting revenue. For the next 100 years, Panama barely cultivated enough food to support itself and produced little or nothing for export.

The Nineteenth Century

Although Panama was a relatively quiet part of Spanish America, other regions were agitating for independence from Spain. A gulf existed between Spanish-descended colonists—who regarded South America as their homeland—and the Spanish officials sent from Spain. By the early nineteenth century, rebels—such as Simon Bolívar of Venezuela—sought to free the colonies of Spanish rule.

Although a Venezuelan by birth, Simon Bolívar was an important figure in the independence struggles of Panama, Colombia, Ecuador, Peru, and Venezuela.

Courtesy of Inter-American Development Bank

Simon Bolívar's victory at the Battle of Boyacá in 1819 dissolved the Viceroyalty of New Granada and signaled the birth of Gran Colombia, which included present-day Colombia, Ecuador, and Venezuela. Panamanians discussed whether to stay with Colombia or to join their region to Peru's territory. In 1821 they opted to remain a department of Gran Colombia.

Between 1830 and 1840, Panamanians made three attempts to establish their province's independence from Colombia. Each time, the region was reintegrated into Gran Colombia, with the result that Panama and its overseer were frequently at odds.

The California gold rush of the late 1840s restored Panama's prosperity. Because coast-to-coast travel in the United States was difficult, many prospectors sailed from the eastern United States to Panama, crossed the isthmus, and took another ship to California. This traffic produced enormous profits for the Panamanians who provided the travelers with food and services.

In 1850 Colombia permitted a group of U.S. investors to build a railroad across the isthmus to simplify the overland journey. By 1855 workers had completed the Panama Railroad, which linked Panama City on the Pacific side with Colón, a new urban center on the Atlantic side.

Panama's political situation continued to deteriorate, however. Rebellions and violence frequently occurred as Panamanians tried to separate their territory from Colombia. Liberal and conservative governments rose and fell, undoing the work of the previous administration.

Artwork by Laura Westlund

The red and blue colors on the Panamanian national flag represent the liberal and conservative political parties that alternated in power during the nineteenth and twentieth centuries. The white stands for peace between the parties. The blue star symbolizes loyalty, and the red star signifies the authority of the nation's laws.

Photo by Bettmann Archive

A period drawing shows a train on the Panama Railroad in the mid-1850s.

A bust of Ferdinand-Marie de Lesseps—the French engineering genius of the late nineteenth century—stands in the Plaza de Francia in Panama City.

President Theodore Roosevelt was anxious to arrange an agreement for building a canal across Panama and advocated Panama's independence from Colombia in the late nineteenth and early twentieth centuries.

Canal Rights

During this period of political upheaval, foreign interests were setting their sights on building a canal across Panama. Panamanians had discussed such a route several times, but internal unrest and lack of funds prevented the idea from taking shape. Moreover, Colombia and Panama could not agree about who should receive the profits from a trans-isthmian canal.

In 1878 Colombia granted the right to build a canal across Panama to a French adventurer named Lucien Napoleon Bonaparte Wyse. He sold these rights to a French company headed by Ferdinand-Marie de Lesseps, who had directed the construction of the Suez Canal. Lesseps's purchase included the Panama Railroad.

Digging for a canal began in 1883, but Lesseps's company ran out of money six years later. A second French firm, the New Panama Canal Company, took over the property of the bankrupt company in 1894. But the new firm made only minor efforts to continue digging until another buyer could be found.

The United States became interested in connecting the Pacific and Atlantic oceans with a canal because the gold rush had drawn so many people across the isthmus to California. In 1899 the U.S. Congress authorized the Isthmian Canal Commission to survey possible canal routes. Primary among these sites was Panama, where some excavation had been done and where a few French buildings already stood.

The New Panama Canal Company offered to sell its Panama rights and property—as well as the Panama Railroad—to the United States for $40 million. In 1902 the U.S. Congress gave President Theodore Roosevelt permission to accept the French offer only if Colombia granted permanent control of a canal zone to the United States.

To ensure that the commercial benefits of a canal across the isthmus would go to Panama rather than to Colombia, Panamanians revolted against Colombia on

November 3, 1903, and declared their independence. The United States and France had encouraged this move by sending weapons and money to the Panamanians. On November 6, the United States recognized the Republic of Panama.

Less than two weeks later, Panama and the United States signed a treaty that gave the United States control of a 10-mile-wide canal zone. In return for the zone, the United States handed Panama an initial payment of $10 million plus $250,000 a year in revenue. The United States formally took over the New Panama Canal Company's property in May 1904.

A New Nation

Manuel Amador Guerrero, a leader in the movement for Panamanian independence, became the new country's first president.

Independent Picture Service

Panama achieved independence in 1903, and the republic's official coat of arms has elements reminiscent of its history — the swords and guns of pirate raids, the digging tools of canal crews, and the engineering achievement of the Gaillard Cut. Translated, the Latin motto means "For the benefit of the world."

Soon after independence, the Cuna Indians convinced the Panamanian government that they were a separate segment of the population. As a result, the Cuna were able to retain a distinct ethnic identity.

Photo by Dr. Roma Hoff

Under Panama's Constitution of 1904, the United States guaranteed Panama's sovereignty—a move that Colombia's claims to the region had prompted. Eventually, however, this clause—which the United States used to intervene in Panama's affairs—caused bitterness between the two countries.

The new nation experienced some instability in its early years. Cuna Indians rejected local efforts to control their people, and political factions developed. The Cuna eventually established themselves as a semi-independent part of Panama. But political feuding continued among an elite group of wealthy, Spanish-descended families, who had run Panama's internal affairs for decades.

Building the Canal

While Panama dealt with its problems as a new nation, the United States pursued its goal of constructing a canal that would be under its complete control. During the first two years of canal building, workers cleared brush, drained swamps, and cut out large areas of grass where disease-carrying mosquitoes swarmed. Tropical diseases—not engineering concerns—became the greatest obstacles to building the canal. With U.S. medical assistance, yellow fever was eliminated by 1906, and by 1913 the number of deaths caused by malaria had also been reduced.

U.S. engineers believed that a canal with locks (water-filled chambers) would be cheaper and faster to build than a sea-level canal. Moreover, a lock system would more efficiently control the floodwaters of the Chagres River, which flowed through the Canal Zone. George W. Goethals, an army engineer, supervised three major engineering projects: excavating the Gaillard Cut, building a dam across the Chagres River to create Gatun Lake, and constructing the canal's locks.

At the height of activity in 1913, more than 43,000 persons worked on the canal. Three-fourths of the workers were poorly paid Antilleans—black people from British-held Caribbean islands. These laborers received wages amounting to only half of the salaries paid to clerical and skilled employees who came from the United States. In addition, Panamanian society rejected the black workers, who thus did not benefit from political and social changes in the nation.

Theodore Roosevelt appointed George Washington Goethals *(pictured above)* as chief engineer of the Panama Canal project in 1907. Under his capable administration, the canal was completed three years ahead of schedule.

In August 1910 workers and equipment littered the floor of what would become the Pedro Miguel Locks—one of the first steps in a Pacific-to-Atlantic journey through the Panama Canal.

Independent Picture Service

Free—but segregated—public schools were operated for the children of U.S. canal personnel stationed in Panama. In 1904 the Gorgona School for Whites began operation in what would eventually become the Canal Zone.

The main work of building the canal was completed in 1914. On August 15 of that year the SS *Ancon,* a passenger-cargo ship owned by the Panama Railroad Company, made the first complete passage through the canal. The canal had cost the United States about $320 million to construct.

Independent Picture Service

The official seal of the former Canal Zone shows a Spanish galleon plying the waters between the Atlantic and Pacific sides. Since the canal region was formally handed over to the Republic of Panama, the zone has been renamed the Panama Canal Area.

The Early Twentieth Century

Revenues from the Panama Canal brought economic prosperity to Panama early in the twentieth century. Political unrest among rival elite factions, however, remained a problem. By 1920 the United States had intervened four times in the civil life of Panama on the pretext of maintaining Panamanian independence. In 1931, however, U.S. policy changed. In that year, the United States refused to interfere when a nationalist group overthrew the government in a coup d'état (a swift, forceful takeover).

Government corruption and the effects of a worldwide economic depression spurred the coup. Harmodio Arias Madrid, a member of the nationalist group, was elected president in 1932. Arias, who came from a poor, rural family, was the first president to establish relief efforts for rural Panamanians. He also represented a segment of Panamanian society that had become strongly nationalistic and anti-American. Throughout the 1930s, Panamanian and U.S. politicians worked to revise treaty agreements to address some Panamanian concerns, such as proof of their ultimate control over the territory that contained the canal.

In the 1940s the nationalism that had brought Arias to power continued to be a factor in Panama's political life. After World War II (1939–1945), the United States wanted to retain several military bases that it had built in Panama during the global conflict. Clashes over the issue —including an anti-U.S. demonstration of 10,000 Panamanians—prompted the Panamanian national assembly to refuse the U.S. request. This refusal marked the first time that Panama had strongly asserted its rights against U.S. intentions.

Also after the war, political power in Panama shifted to the national police force. Its commander, José Remón, installed and removed Panamanian presidents until his own election as chief executive in 1952. By increasing salaries and modernizing weap-

After eight years of dredging, building, and disease, the SS *Ancon*—a passenger-cargo vessel owned by the Panama Railroad Company—became the first ship officially to make the journey from the Atlantic Ocean to the Pacific Ocean via the Panama Canal.

ons, Remón turned the police into a military force and renamed it the National Guard. Although he grew wealthy as president, Remón also used his authority to enact economic and social reforms and to promote industrial development. His reforms were short-lived, however. In 1955 Remón was assassinated, and a vice president completed his term of office.

Relations with the United States

In 1951 the U.S. Congress changed the name of the Panama Railroad Company to the Panama Canal Company and gave it control of the canal. The company oversaw the maintenance of the canal and organized facilities for canal employees.

In the late 1950s Panamanians grew increasingly unhappy over U.S. control of the Canal Zone. They wanted a greater share in its administration for themselves. Riots over the U.S. presence broke out in 1959. Some Panamanians tried to force their way into the Canal Zone to raise the Panamanian flag as a symbol of territorial authority. Hundreds of U.S. troops met the protesters at the zone's border.

A year later, the United States avoided more disorder by arranging for U.S. and Panamanian flags to fly side by side in one place in the zone to signify Panama's sovereignty. In 1962 the United States agreed to let both flags appear together throughout the zone. To further answer Panamanian complaints, the United States

In the mid-twentieth century, con-
flicts arose between the United
States and Panama over control of
the Canal Zone. Symbolic of the disagreements were the placement and
flying of national flags. In the early
1970s both U.S. and Panamanian
flags flew side by side at Balboa
Heights—when Balboa was still administrative headquarters of the
U.S.-governed Panama Canal Zone—
to underscore Panama's sovereignty
over its national territory.

Independent Picture Service

raised the wages of Panamanians employed
by the Panama Canal Company to be equal
to salaries of U.S. workers. The United
States also gave financial aid to encourage
Panamanian businesses in the Canal Zone.

Riots broke out again between Panamanians and U.S. citizens in 1964. Some
students in the Canal Zone were against
the policy that arranged for the flags of
both nations to fly together. They tried to

Photo by UPI/Bettmann Newsphotos

In 1964 Panamanian students demonstrated against U.S. control of the Panama Canal. The banner they carry translates
to say, "The Canal Is Ours."

raise the U.S. emblem alone over their school. Word of this gesture reached Panamanian students, who brought their national flag with them to the zone. In the fighting that followed, 4 U.S. soldiers and about 20 Panamanians died. At the root of the 1964 riots was the local feeling that the United States had used the canal arrangements to take advantage of the strategically placed nation.

Following the confrontation in the zone, President Roberto F. Chiari, who had been elected in 1960, severed relations and charged the United States with aggression. Regional meetings restored diplomatic ties between the two countries, but the canal issue still caused bitterness in Panama.

When Marco Aurelio Robles was elected to succeed Chiari in 1964, U.S. president Lyndon B. Johnson stated that the United States would negotiate a new canal treaty. In June 1967 Presidents Johnson and

Robles announced that drafts of three new documents had been drawn up to replace the 1903 agreement. But opposition to the new treaties mounted in Panama, and the Panamanian president declared that further talks were needed to iron out disagreements between the two nations.

Control by the National Guard

In addition to problems in the zone, Panama experienced difficulties with its system of government in the 1960s. For decades, an elite group of wealthy politicians had shared the job of running Panama. This arrangement left middle- and low-income citizens without power. In the elections of 1968, the fairness of the election process became an issue. With the backing of the National Guard—a necessity to win an election—Arnulfo Arias Madrid became president. Within a few months, however, the guard had removed

Photo by UPI/Bettmann Newsphotos

Marco Robles became president of Panama in 1964 and supported U.S. efforts to negotiate new canal treaties.

Photo by UPI/Bettmann Newsphotos

In the late 1960s, Omar Torrijos came to power as head of Panama's National Guard. He ran the government unofficially until 1972, when the Panamanian legislature named him the country's president.

Arias because he had tried to weaken the guard's hold on the political life of Panama.

The 1968 overthrow of Arias led to the military's open domination of the Panamanian government. After the coup, the National Guard set up a two-person junta (council) to rule Panama. The guard also disbanded the national assembly, banned all political parties, and arrested hundreds of political leaders. Eventually, General Omar Torrijos Herrera, commander of the National Guard, became the dictator of Panama, despite the junta's appointment of a civilian president.

The junta announced that legislative elections would take place in 1972. In that year Panama also put into effect a new constitution, which greatly expanded the government's powers. After the elections, the 505-member assembly confirmed Torrijos as president.

With dictatorial authority, Torrijos enacted reforms. He sponsored the construction of schools, health facilities, roads, and bridges in rural areas. These moves made him popular among Panamanians.

Torrijos also tackled the problem of the stalled treaty negotiations for the canal. Changing the 1903 agreement with the United States became central to his goals for the nation, principally because so much of Panama's economy was dependent on the operation of the canal.

New Canal Treaties

After several false starts, U.S. and Panamanian negotiators met in 1976 to discuss

Courtesy of Museum of Modern Art of Latin America

U.S. president Jimmy Carter (left) and Panama's chief executive Omar Torrijos (right) listen to remarks by Alejandro Orfila (center), secretary general of the Organization of American States (OAS). Orfila spoke during ceremonies celebrating the signing of the 1977 Panama Canal treaties at OAS headquarters in Washington, D.C.

Although political power in Panama is concentrated in the hands of the head of the Panama Defense Forces, there is an elected civilian chief executive of the Republic of Panama. The president resides in a mansion, which is known locally as *Palacio de las Garzas* (Palace of the Herons), because live herons play in a large fountain located near the entrance of the residence in Panama City.

new arrangements for operating the canal. Encouraging the process were other nations in the Western Hemisphere—such as Venezuela, Costa Rica, and Jamaica— who urged that a fairer treaty be drawn up. These various efforts produced a new, two-part document, which Torrijos and U.S. president Jimmy Carter signed in September 1977. Under the new treaties, control of the canal and the Canal Zone would be transferred to Panama by the year 2000. Despite some political opposition to the new drafts, the Panamanian people and the U.S. Congress approved both treaties in 1978.

The first treaty transferred legal authority over the canal to Panama and established a Panama Canal Commission, which will maintain the canal until December 31, 1999. On that date, Panama will take over ownership and management.

Five U.S. citizens and four Panamanians make up the commission.

The second treaty guaranteed that the canal would be open to peaceful transit by vessels of all nations at all times. This second agreement allows the United States to intervene if the canal's safety is threatened but provides for joint Panamanian and U.S. responsibility for the canal's protection until 1999.

New economic initiatives accompanied the canal treaties. Torrijos enacted laws that were designed to make Panama a financial hub in Latin America. These new arrangements made it easy for foreigners to deposit funds—sometimes secretly—in Panamanian bank accounts because regulations protected the identity of depositors. As investors became aware of these laws, a number of additional banks opened in Panama City. Some of the banks

In 1988—following the imposition of economic penalties by the United States—Panamanians objected to the government's decision to close the nation's banks. Here, retired workers wave their pension checks in frustration.

Photo by Reuters/Bettmann Newsphotos

accepted deposits from illegal drug traffickers, who distributed cocaine and marijuana throughout the region.

Recent Events

Torrijos died in a plane crash in 1981, and senior members of the National Guard (renamed the Panama Defense Forces, PDF) vied for power. By 1983 General Manuel Noriega—head of the PDF—became Panama's behind-the-scenes dictator. In 1985, for example, Noriega forced President Nicolás Ardito Barletta Vallarino to resign because Barletta had suggested that Noriega and the PDF were involved in the death of a Panamanian political leader.

Under Noriega's influence, banks continued to attract huge deposits of money. By the mid-1980s, Panamanian banks had assets of $40 billion. Noriega became personally wealthy as a result of large sums paid to him by drug traffickers. These dealers wanted to use Panama as an illegal base of operations and to disguise the source of their huge incomes.

In 1987 Roberto Díaz Herrera, Noriega's second in command in the PDF, accused Noriega of participating in drug trafficking, election fraud, and the murder of political rivals. Opposition groups in Panama staged strikes and demonstrations against Noriega's corrupt regime. As a result of the uprisings, Noriega declared a state of emergency, which allowed him to ban public protests and to restrict civil liberties.

Meanwhile, drug enforcement agents from the United States began investigating Noriega. They suspected him of taking payoffs from drug traffickers, who sent their illegal goods into the United States by way of Panama. Although U.S. administrations had supported dictatorships in Panama, renewed efforts to stem the drug flow prompted the U.S. government to try to force Noriega out of power. The United States cut off $26 million in annual aid to Panama, a move that created serious economic problems for Panama. Nevertheless, Noriega remained in charge of Panamanian affairs.

In 1988 Panama's president, Eric Arturo Delvalle Henríquez, ordered Noriega to be removed as head of the PDF. Instead, the Panamanian legislature supported Noriega and dismissed Delvalle. Manuel Solís

Palma, the minister of education, took over the presidency. (The United States continues to recognize Delvalle as Panama's president.)

Panamanians took to the streets to protest against the severe economic conditions. Noriega's PDF stopped the demonstrations and strikes and tried to crush political opposition. Noriega continued to maintain his hold on power, although Panama's economy—worsened by additional economic sanctions applied in mid-1988—was rapidly deteriorating.

Government

In practice, the commander of the PDF exercises supreme power in Panama. Politicians who have national or local authority possess it with the approval of the commander of the PDF.

The formal governmental structure of Panama is comprised of executive, legislative, and judicial branches. The offices of president and vice president were filled in 1984 by direct popular election for the first time since 1972. Under Panama's constitution, the president is elected for a five-year term and appoints a cabinet to assist in governing the nation.

The legislative branch of Panama's government was changed in 1984. The national assembly and the national legislative council that had been established by the Constitution of 1972 were dissolved. These organizations were replaced by a unicameral (one-house) legislative assembly. Voters elect the 67 members of this law-making body to five-year terms.

The president names the justices of the supreme court, who serve 10-year terms. There are nine judges, and their appointments are subject to the approval of the legislative assembly.

For administrative purposes, Panama is divided into nine provinces. A governor heads each province, but local officials generally do not have much authority. Their job is to carry out the policies of the national government.

General Manuel Noriega *(left)* gives a power salute from the balcony of the presidential palace after installing Manuel Solís Palma *(right)* as president in February 1988.

Photo by Reuters/Bettmann Newsphotos

Cuna Indians of the San Blas Islands form close family ties. This fact—along with their remote location and dislike of mainland lifestyles—gives them the strength to remain culturally distinct from the Panamanian mainstream. In their isolated existence, the Cuna are able to hand down their intricate sewing skills from generation to generation.

Courtesy of Leanne Hogie

3) The People

The population of the Republic of Panama—2.3 million in 1988—is one of the smallest in Latin America. Growing annually at a rate of 2.2 percent, the population will double in about 32 years. Approximately 40 percent of the nation live in either Panama City or Colón, which lie at opposite ends of the canal.

Not included in Panama's population, but dwelling within the nation's boundaries, are U.S. civilian and military personnel in the Canal Area. In the mid-1980s there were over 30,000 U.S. citizens living in Panama.

Recent hostilities between General Noriega and the United States have caused some of the dependents of U.S. workers to return home. Members of the military are part of the U.S. Southern Command—a 10,000-person force stationed in Panama that goes on maneuvers throughout Latin America.

Ethnic Origins

The Indians, who are descended from the original inhabitants of the country, currently number about 100,000. They are divided into three major groups: the Guaymí, the Cuna, and the Chocó. The Guaymí live in the northwestern part of the nation near Costa Rica, the Cuna reside in the San Blas territory along the Atlantic coast, and the Chocó dwell inland from the Pacific coast in the southeast. Each group lives according to its own traditions and generally governs itself. The Indians form a separate culture within Panama and have a political status that is distinct from the rest of Panamanians.

Most of the Guaymí, who make up 50 percent of the entire Indian population, speak their own dialect. They support themselves by hunting and fishing, and many, especially the women, grow tobacco, fruit, corn, and rice in small fields. The men often work as herders or agricultural laborers on nearby estates.

The Cuna constitute about 42 percent of the Indian population, and nearly half of them are bilingual in Spanish and their

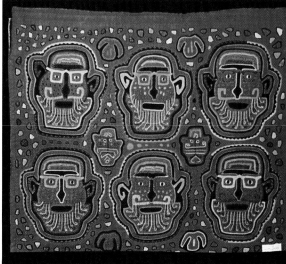

Courtesy of Museum of Modern Art of Latin America

Molas are distinctive and beautiful textiles sewn by Cuna Indian women. Each mola illustrates an original theme or image – such as this view of six male faces.

own dialect. They seem to have the best chance of retaining their cultural identity, partly because they live in the isolated San Blas Islands of northern Panama. They also maintain a closely knit community life

Courtesy of Leanne Hogie

The Cuna still use traditional dugout canoes to move both people and goods from island to island in the San Blas Archipelago.

41

that protects them from outside influences. The Cuna are opposed to becoming part of the Panamanian mainstream.

The Chocó occupy a region of Darién province near Colombia and represent only 8 percent of all Indian groups. They have often intermarried with Spanish-speaking blacks.

The Spanish-speaking Roman Catholics constitute the majority of the country's people. Seventy percent of them are mestizos—people of mixed European and Indian ancestry.

A third group consists of English-speaking, Protestant blacks, called Antilleans. Their ancestors came from Caribbean islands under British control to work on the construction of the trans-isthmian railway and the canal.

The Antilleans generally are not accepted as members of Panamanian society.

This situation arose partly because Antilleans do not participate in the dominant Spanish-speaking and Catholic culture. Most Antilleans live in Panama City, Colón, or the Canal Area. They constitute about 8 percent of the population, but their numbers are declining, since fewer Antilleans are emigrating to Panama.

There are also groups of East Indians and Chinese who tend to cling to their own languages and customs. Spanish is the official language of the country, but many Panamanians also speak English, especially those who work in the Canal Area.

Daily Life

In rural areas, most farmers live in one-story houses with thatched roofs, walls of bamboo or dried sugarcane, dirt floors, and bamboo ceilings. Rural residents are poor,

Independent Picture Service

While joining in a community effort to build a village home, friends take a break to play a game that involves arm wrestling in the mud.

42

Avenida Central is a major thorough-fare in Panama City. Lined with signs in Spanish and English, the avenue runs west from Panamá Viejo, through downtown Panama City, and out beyond Independence Plaza. Many of the buildings have corru-gated-iron or clay-tile roofs.

own little furniture, and sleep on wooden cots. Boxes or tree stumps often serve as tables or chairs. Urban dwellers live in houses and apartment buildings made of wood or concrete, with roofs of clay tiles or corrugated iron.

Most Panamanians wear light, loose clothing suitable for the tropics. Dressing in the national costume is reserved for fiestas (feast days) and other special occasions. The pollera, or women's costume, is a long, full dress made of many folds of fine white cotton, decorated with delicate

Putting on a *pollera* – the women's national costume in Panama – requires time and effort. The billowing white dress embroidered with lively floral designs – usually in bright pink, green, or blue – is complemented by gold and pearl hair ornaments (*tembleque*) and gold-embellished combs. Earrings and long strands of pearls complete the costume, which is worn on special holidays.

43

The golden altar in the church of San José was painted black by a resourceful monk in the seventeenth century to disguise it during Henry Morgan's attack on the old city.

Education

By law all children between the ages of 7 and 15 must attend school. About 89 percent of Panamanian children of primary school age are enrolled in school, but only about 60 percent of the children of secondary school age attend high school. Twenty-three percent of the population between the ages of 20 and 24 are enrolled in higher education. After health and housing, the government spends about 11 percent of its expenditures on education. About 88 percent of the population are literate. The government operates free elementary and secondary schools, as well as a teachers' college. The University of Panama, founded in 1935, has a fine campus in Panama City.

Health

Health conditions in Panama are generally good, except in urban slum areas where

lace and embroidery. Men wear the *montuno*, a costume made of coarse white cotton. It includes a loose, long-sleeved embroidered shirt worn over short, fringed trousers.

About 93 percent of Panamanians are Roman Catholics. Almost every town or village holds a colorful fiesta every year in honor of its patron saint. In urban areas, Carnival is celebrated during the four days preceding the beginning of Lent, when Panamanians take part in dances, parties, and parades. Panama's chief sports include baseball, horse racing, boxing, swimming, fishing, and hunting.

Panamanian family life is grounded in Hispanic traditions. In most families, the mother's responsibilities focus on the home and on relations within the family. The father deals with business outside the household, although he considers himself its undisputed head.

Panamanian girls make up a significant portion of the total enrollment in primary and secondary schools. Once beyond high school, students have good opportunities—especially in urban areas—to pursue further education.

Activity in the library at the University of Panama illustrates the avid interest of Panamanians in furthering their education. With a student body of about 35,000 – including the enrollment at five regional campuses – the university is making an attempt to bring higher learning to those who desire it.

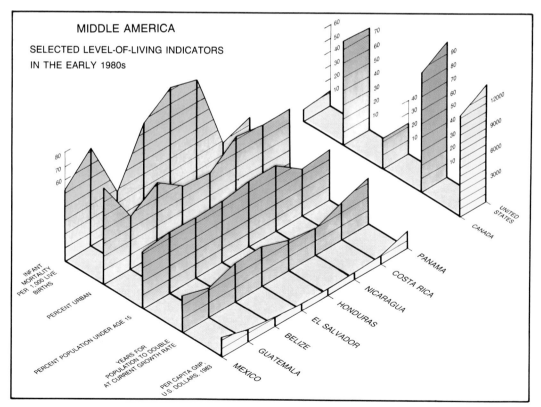

This graph shows how each of five factors, which are suggestive of the quality and style of life, varies among the eight Middle American countries. Canada and the United States are included for comparison. Data from "1986 World Population Data Sheet" (Washington, D.C.: Population Reference Bureau, Inc., 1986).

45

In Los Santos province of southern Panama, one of the residents of the town of Llano Largo fills a tub from a water tap recently installed at her home. Until the new water system was constructed, her family had to carry all their water from a public pump more than a block away.

tuberculosis and other diseases are still common. Government-sponsored health programs provide free medical examinations for low-income Panamanians. The government also promotes education on preventive health care and on the importance of good sanitation practices.

Panamanians tend to live longer than most Central Americans. The national life expectancy figure is 71 years, compared to an average of 66 years for the rest of the region. In the mid-1980s there were about 1,250 patients for every physician in Panama, a higher rate than in other Central American countries. The infant mortality rate—25 per 1,000 live births—is the lowest after Costa Rica. In urban areas 75 percent of the homes have access to safe water, but this proportion falls to less than 10 percent in rural Panama.

The Arts

Panama has a rich folk culture, which Panamanians at all levels of society enjoy. The country's folk music reflects Spanish, West Indian, African, and even North American influences.

The *mejorana* is a folk song probably imported from Spain in the eighteenth century. It can be either vocal or instrumental but is seldom used for dancing. The national folk dances are the tamborito and the *cumbia*. Couples perform the cumbia in a rotating circle to the sound of maracas (pebble-filled gourds) and drums. The dance reputedly mimics the behavior of the colonial Spaniards and was brought to the area with the African slave trade. The tamborito is also a dance with an old Afro-Spanish history. It was popular in seventeenth-century Spain and is based on

African rhythms. The tamborito is performed to clapping hands and several drums. Both dances are traditionally seen during fiestas and Carnival festivities throughout Panama.

Nationalism has been the major theme of most Panamanian literature. Ramón Valdés published *Independence of the Isthmus of Panama* just after the country freed itself from Colombia. His work became the basis for most of the historical treatises that followed. Ricardo Miró became the national poet during this same period, and his work, "Patria" (fatherland), inspired both schoolchildren and adults with feelings of national unity.

After independence, the national government promoted cultural pursuits. It founded the first national music conservatory and helped to build the National Theater. Panama's rich cultural life now centers on the Panamanian Art Institute, the National Institute of Music, and schools that focus on instruction in music, art, dance, and theater. Traveling musical groups and drama companies—as well as artists and poets—bring cultural events to residents throughout the nation.

Food

Rice, the chief food in Panama, is served either plain or mixed with meat and vegetables. Maize and beans are also important in the national diet. Women grind maize into a paste from which they make tortillas—very thin pancakes. Coffee is the most common beverage.

A wide variety of dishes prepared in the republic are distinctly Panamanian. One is Panama's traditional soup, *sancocho*. The soup is prepared by stewing chicken, yucca (a palmlike plant having edible fruit), otoe (a local root), corn, plantains (a starchy, bananalike plant), and potatoes. *Sopa borracha* is a rich sponge cake soaked in rum and garnished with raisins and prunes that have been marinated in sherry.

Because Panama borders two oceans, the national diet is rich in fish and shellfish. One well-known dish is seviche, usually made by combining corbina (sea bass) with tiny red and yellow peppers and onions sliced paper-thin. The mixture is marinated overnight in lemon juice, oil, and seasonings and is usually eaten raw as an appetizer or a snack.

With Panama's extensive coastlines, the national diet is rich in seafood. Here, a crew pulls heavy nets to shore.

A Panamanian farmer cultivates a cantaloupe field with a Japanese-built tractor near Parita in southern Panama. About 33 percent of the nation's work force is engaged in agriculture, even though farm production has decreased in importance when compared to the nation's overall production of goods and services.

4) The Economy

Thirty-three percent of Panama's economically active population are involved in agriculture. Roughly 60 percent work in business, manufacturing, public administration, transportation, and communications. The Panama Canal is an important factor in the republic's economic life, partly because the Canal Area provides jobs for workers employed by the Panama Canal Commission. Some of the charges levied on ships passing through the canal go into the national treasury. In addition, Panamanian companies also sell food and other supplies to the ships that pass through the canal.

Agriculture

Most Panamanian farmers cultivate one or two acres of land with simple tools. The

The health of Panama's economy is heavily dependent on its canal, which operates 24 hours a day.

Large banana plantations are found throughout fertile Chiriquí province. Here, ripe clusters are being wrapped in plastic bags, before being transported to a packing plant or refrigerated cargo ship.

The ultrarich soil of the highlands of Chiriquí province in western Panama produces most of the nation's food, making the area the breadbasket of the republic.

49

A wide variety of fruits and vegetables grows well in the Chiriquí Highlands. Here, farmers tend a huge field of cabbages.

crops tend to be consumed by those who produce them. Since World War II, large landowners, living mainly in Coclé and Chiriquí provinces, have increased production by using modern farm machinery. Of 92,000 recorded plots of land, roughly half are smaller than 10 acres. On the other hand, half of the 5.2 million acres under cultivation are owned by 3 percent of the landowning farmers.

Rice is the chief crop, and its production is encouraged by the government. Large farms using machinery, fertilizers, and better seeds have increased yields to more than one ton per acre. On smaller farms, yields run less than a third of a ton per acre. Corn and beans are other basic crops,

Maize is among the popular, easily grown crops that thrive on small acreages.

grown mostly on small farms that do not use modern technology.

Bananas are an important cash crop in Panama, and they have remained the nation's most important export over the years. United Brands, formerly the United Fruit Company, accounts for most of the banana exports. Another crop occupying large areas of land is sugarcane. Cane, like other crops, is subject to price fluctuations reflecting changing patterns of world supply and demand. Consequently, the Panamanian sugar industry continues to face serious difficulties, even though the government has tried to help by building state-owned refining mills.

Citrus fruits, mangoes, coffee, maize, cacao, tobacco, vegetables, coconuts, and potatoes are also grown, often on small acreages. Coffee, for example, is grown on farms averaging under three acres in size, mainly in Chiriquí province.

Independent Picture Service

Citrus fruits, such as these oranges that are being harvested by workers on ladders, also flourish in Panama's fertile highlands.

Courtesy of Minneapolis Public Library and Information Center

Large banana groves are generally managed by corporations like United Brands, which, by itself, accounts for most of Panama's banana exports.

51

Livestock raising has been increasing in importance, contributing over one-fourth of all agricultural output. Cattle raising for both meat and milk is common in the provinces of Chiriquí, Los Santos, and Veraguas. Most ranches cover about 200 acres, although a few are much larger. Cattle are fed almost entirely on grass.

Energy and Industry

Industrial growth in Panama has been restricted by the country's lack of natural resources, particularly fuels such as oil and coal. Firewood was the traditional fuel in use, but cutting has led to the clearing of much forested land. Bagasse (a by-product of sugar manufacturing) is employed in the sugar refineries for drying.

Until 1976, when hydroelectric power came into use, Panama had to depend heavily on imported oil to generate electricity. By the mid-1980s most power was being generated by hydroelectric plants located along the nation's rivers. The La Fortuna plant, opened in 1984, almost doubled

Courtesy of David Mangurian

Relaxed and at home in the saddle, this Panamanian cowboy works on a ranch where brahma cattle are raised. In recent years cattle raising has become an important economic activity in Panama.

In addition to abundant agricultural potential, Chiriquí province, along with the provinces of Los Santos and Veraguas, hosts successful livestock-breeding operations.

When it is completed, this hydroelectric plant in Chiriquí will consist of a 197-foot-tall dam, a 230-foot-tall water-powered intake tower, 30 miles of roads, 10 miles of tunnels, and a powerhouse 1,312 feet inside a mountain. The dam site is supervised by a U.S. engineering firm, whose representative *(left)* is talking with the Panamanian engineer responsible for building the powerhouse.

Using locally produced leather, employees at Industria Chitreana de Calzados in Herrera province make high-quality shoes that require a substantial amount of hand labor. This factory—the first of its kind in Panama—employs about 50 people who together produce approximately 200 pairs of shoes a day.

Sausages are carefully racked at a plant in La Arena. Food processing is an industry of increasing importance in Panama.

the proportion of Panama's energy needs that are supplied by hydropower.

The leading industries of Panama are cement manufacturing, sugar refining, fish processing, and oil refining. Many of the processing plants operate in Panama City and Colón—the nation's chief industrial areas. Small factories and shops produce pottery, clothing, furniture, shoes, soap, soft drinks, and alcoholic beverages. People in rural areas use leather, wood, gourds, and fibrous materials to make useful articles such as saddles, mats, baskets, kitchen utensils, and containers.

Fishing and Forestry

Fishing contributes significantly to Panama's economy. Many kinds of fish, as well as lobster and shrimp, are found in the nation's coastal waters. Shrimp farming, also called aquaculture, is a successful industry and provides almost one-fifth of Panama's annual export earnings. Panama also has

Courtesy of Inter-American Development Bank

Farmers load produce from their newly harvested fields onto a truck for transport to markets in Panama City. As each new stretch of the Pan-American Highway is completed, farmers follow to settle and plant crops on the previously unreachable land.

Courtesy of Inter-American Development Bank

A worker makes plastic bags at Plastinic de Panamá in Panama City. Plastic bags are a boon in preserving food and meats in the tropics.

55

two fishmeal plants, which process anchovies and herring for international markets.

Although vast forests—especially of mahogany—exist in Panama, they generally remain untapped. In the mid-1980s, 80 percent of the harvested wood was used as fuel. With only a few roads into thickly forested areas, Panamanians cannot reach and remove this resource. Only timber near river routes is being harvested.

Nearly all of the country's forests are government-owned, and, of these, about three-fourths are tropical rain-forests. Care must be taken when clearing a rain-forest, since the region's ecological balance will be damaged by cutting too many trees. Uncontrolled harvesting can lead to soil erosion because there are fewer plant roots to hold the soil in place.

Courtesy of United Nations

Seafood—particularly shrimp—is among Panama's main exports. Here, hand-nets are thrown to collect plankton, which is used as nourishment for farm-raised shrimp.

Independent Picture Service

Groves of teak trees, which have strong, water-resistant wood, thrive in Panama's tropical climate.

Banks and high-rise apartment buildings share Panama City's skyline. There are more financial institutions per capita in Panama than in any other country, and the banks do a thriving business thanks to lenient deposit laws and a high level of confidentiality.

Trade and Banking

Panama's chief exports are bananas, refined petroleum products, shrimp, and sugar. Other commodities that are shipped abroad include coconuts, cattle hides, cacao, and abaca (a fiber made from banana stalks). Aside from lumber, forest products for export include sarsaparilla (a pungent extract from the root of the smilax plant) and rotenone (an insect poison made from the root of the cubé plant).

Imports include petroleum for refining, transshipment, and domestic use; transportation equipment; chemicals; foodstuffs; and a variety of consumer goods. The United States buys most of Panama's exports and supplies more than half of the country's imports.

The development of Panama's financial services has provided a new source of economic opportunity in recent years. Panama's high interest rates—along with laws that make it easy for foreign depositors to maintain secret accounts—have brought a flood of foreign capital into Panamanian banks. Banking profits make up almost 10 percent of Panama's gross national product (the amount of goods and services produced in a year) and are an important aspect of the nation's economy.

57

When three small sections of the Pan-American Highway in Panama are completed, the entire Western Hemisphere will be connected by road, from Alaska to the southern tip of Chile. This newly paved section is near Tocumen, east of Panama City.

Courtesy of Inter-American Development Bank

Also attractive to foreigners are Panama's laws governing corporations. Lenient regulations allow tax-free companies to be formed in Panama. In addition, the manner in which these companies make money—as well as who owns them—remains secret. These firms are called "shell companies," and investors often use them to hide taxable assets generated in other countries.

Some banks have been accused of laundering money—that is, of making illicitly acquired funds appear to be legitimate by funneling them through the accounts of legal companies. For example, a fake—but legal—company may be registered in Panama, and bank accounts in the name of that company may be opened to take advantage of Panama's financial secrecy laws. Funds from illegal activities, such as drug trafficking, may be transferred into or withdrawn from these accounts. Estimates indicate that as much as $500 million in illegal money is transferred through Panama's banks every year.

In the mid-1980s the United States charged that, under General Manuel Noriega, Panama had become a major center for laundering drug money. In response to U.S. pressure, Panama's legislature passed a law in 1987 that required banks to provide information about suspected drug dealers and that permitted the freezing of secret bank accounts.

Transportation

In the mid-1980s Panama had about 6,000 miles of roads. The thoroughfare from Panama City westward to David, La Concepción, and the Costa Rican border is part of the Pan-American Highway. This road is completely paved and begins near the Pacific entrance to the canal. The highway crosses Puente de las Américas—a steel-arched bridge that is high enough to permit ships to pass under it. A concrete highway, sometimes called the world's shortest transcontinental road, runs between Panama City and Colón.

The Panama Railroad runs through the Canal Area. It connects Ancón on the Pacific with Cristobal on the Atlantic. Since most vessels bringing goods into Panama unload their cargo at Cristobal near Colón, much of the merchandise going to Panama City is brought overland by the Panama Railroad. United Brands and the Chiriquí National Railroad also operate short railway lines.

Several international airlines fly into Tocumen Airport, which is located 17 miles from Panama City. Local companies provide flights to New York, Los Angeles, Miami, and South American nations, as

Courtesy of Pan American Airways
The mile-long **Puente de las Américas** is near the Pacific end of the still-unfinished Pan-American Highway.

Up to 1980, the highest canal toll was paid by the *Queen Elizabeth 2* on her seventh transit. The ship's toll, which was assessed by net tonnage, was $89,154.62.

59

well as service within Panama and Central America.

Panama's merchant marine is one of the largest in the world, although most of its vessels are owned by shipping lines of other countries. About 700 ships fly the Panamanian flag. Many companies register their vessels in Panama because the country allows them to impose lower taxes than do most other nations. Cristobal and Balboa are Panama's chief ports.

The Canal's Economic Importance

Before the 1977 treaties, the canal provided Panama with limited benefits. The Canal Zone imported most of its goods from the United States without paying an import fee. Most jobs in the canal facilities went to U.S. citizens, and Panama received only a small share of the canal's revenues. Indeed, toll rates were the same for 60 years—from the opening of the canal in 1914 until 1974—when variable rates went into effect. The recent treaties significantly improved Panama's control of and access to canal revenues.

Until the Panamanians assume complete control of the canal in 1999, Panama will receive an annual fixed sum of $10 million from the Panama Canal Commission. The nation is also paid a contingency payment of up to an additional $10 million from unbudgeted, surplus commis-

Independent Picture Service

Since the signing of the canal treaties in 1977, the Panamanian government has acquired substantial assets, such as the pier facilities and bunkering services at Balboa Harbor.

Cristobal—with its vast docking facilities—is said to be the finest port south of the continental United States.

sion profits and 30 cents for each ton of shipping that passes through the canal. These fees can be adjusted for inflation. Panama receives another $10 million annually for the services it provides, including police and fire protection, street cleaning, traffic management, and garbage collection in the Canal Area.

In the early 1980s tolls were set at $1.83 per ton for vessels carrying passengers or cargo. War vessels, hospital ships, and supply boats paid $1.02 per ton. Approximately 12,000 oceangoing vessels travel through the Panama Canal every year— an average of almost 35 a day. Besides ships that are registered in Panama, the most frequent users of the waterway are boats flying the flags of Liberia, Greece, the United States, Great Britain, Ecuador, and the Soviet Union. Although the canal

is an important link in worldwide commerce, rising operating costs and decreased traffic have caused income from the canal to drop in recent years.

The Future

By the year 2000, Panama is expected to receive $60 million to $70 million annually from canal operations. Traffic through the sea-lane fluctuates, however. For example, ships that are too large to use the locks are carrying an increasing amount of the world's freight. This fact may cause a decline in the waterway's use unless canal operators can find a way to accommodate wider vessels.

Because of recent U.S. sanctions, Panama's economy is in serious trouble. Moreover, the relationship between the two

Ships of the U.S. Navy can use the canal for transit and the naval facilities—such as Rodman Naval Station—for repairs.

nations is strained because of disagreements with Noriega over his role in Panama's political life. Indeed, many Panamanians have supported U.S. efforts to oust the general. For the remainder of the twentieth century, however, the successful operation of the canal—Panama's main source of foreign income—will depend on peaceful Panamanian-U.S. relations.

In 1988 looters took items from the ruins of a department store in Panama City. The building caught fire when unpaid public employees burned the car of a Noriega supporter in front of the store.

Military ships from many nations annually pass through the locks. The USS *Iowa* was refitted as a "panamax"—a ship that uses the maximum width of the canal—and has only a small amount of room to spare on either side.

Index